W9-DEG-613

KITES

Barrie Caldecott

Consultant: Henry Pluckrose

Photography: Chris Fairclough

FRANKLIN WATTS
New York/London/Sydney/Toronto

Copyright © 1990 Franklin Watts

Franklin Watts Inc.
387 Park Avenue South
New York
NY 10016

Library of Congress Cataloging-in-Publication Data

Caldecott, Barrie.
    Kites / Barrie Caldecott.
        p.   cm. — (Fresh start)
    Summary: Text and photographs introduce kite designs and the best
material for constructing efficient kites.
    ISBN 0-531-14075-X
    1. Kites—Juvenile literature.   [1. Kites.]   I. Title.
TL759.5.C34   1990
629.133'32—dc20   90-12133
                                                                    CIP AC

Design: K & Co

Editor: Jenny Wood

Typeset by Lineage Ltd,
Watford, England

Printed in Belgium

Contents

Equipment and materials

This book describes activities which use the following:

Adhesives (UHU, Bostik)
Cardboard
Compass
Cutting board
Drill bit (2mm)
Eyelets
Felt-tip pens (permanent, a selection of colors)
File (small)
Flying line, 300 ft (polyester braided, 20-50lb breaking strain)
Gloves
Hacksaw (small)
Hand drill
Hole punch

Line tensioners (or buttons)
Masking tape
Modeling knife
Pencil
Pin
Plastic or paper cup (disposable)
Plastic sheet (lightweight, colored – for example, trash can liners, shopping bags)
Plastic sheet (silver, Mylar or Melinex)
Plastic tubing (clear, flexible, 5mm and 6mm internal diameter)
Ramin dowels (¼ in diameter)
Reel (or handle)
Rubber
Ruler
Sandpaper
Scissors
Set square
Spray mount (spray adhesive)
Sticky tape (1in wide, clear and colored)
Straight edge (3 ft)
Swivel clips
Tape measure
Thread (strong)
Tissue paper (a selection of colors)
Towing rings
Pinwheels (two, paper or plastic, hand-held)

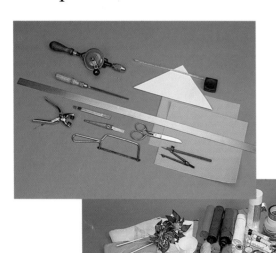

Getting ready

Kite flying is an increasingly popular and enjoyable pastime. One of the great pleasures in life is, on a sunny day, to feel the tug on the line of a kite you have made, as it soars into the sky displaying your mastery of the wind. This book will show you how to make and fly some colorful kites.

The book is arranged so that the simplest kites are presented first. The more complicated designs follow. The six kites chosen illustrate the various stages in the development of the craft of kite-making. The Paper Serpent and the Patchwork Three-stick Hexagonal are based on ancient designs, and are made in the traditional materials of paper and wood. The Bat Box and the Silver Eddy are designs from the 19th century, while the Stained Glass Sled and the Frilly Delta are both modern, flexible kites.

Accuracy and symmetry are most important when making a kite: when hanging from its towing ring, a kite should have perfect balance. To prevent accidents, round the ends of all spars with sandpaper. Sticky tape holds the spars to the plastic sheet very well, and makes the assembly of the kites quick and simple. Strips of sticky tape can also repair any tears that might occur in the kite fabric. (An old kite can develop a new character when it is covered with many tape repairs!) The two paper kites (the Paper Serpent and the Patchwork Three-stick Hexagonal) can also be built using plastic sheet and following the techniques of assembly as described for the Frilly Delta and the Bat Box. Ask an adult to help you drill the holes in the ramin dowels for the Bat Box and the Silver Eddy. You will need help, too, when using the spray adhesive for decorating the paper kites.

Knots

You will need to be able to tie the knots shown in photographs **1-5.** Some of these knots may be familiar, but others you may need to practice!

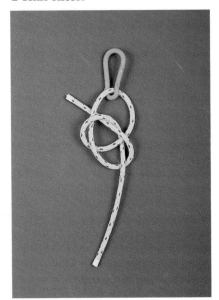

1 Half hitch

3 Reef

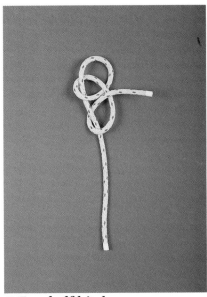

2 Two half hitches

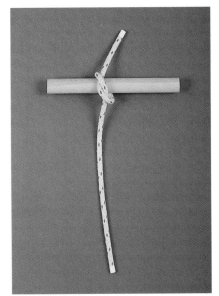

4 Bowline

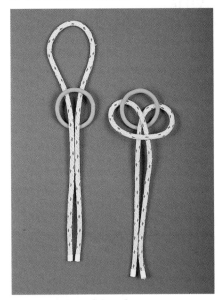

5 Lark's head hitch

Flying the Kites

Before you get your kite airborne, there are certain things you need to know about safety, wind conditions, suitable places to fly, and adjustments that can be made to the kite.

SAFETY

1 Don't fly near electric wires or pylons.

2 Don't fly on wet or rainy days.

3 Don't fly near roads or airports.

4 Don't fly above 500 feet. This is the legal limit, set at this level to keep your kite from colliding with low-flying aircraft.

5 Look out for bystanders if your kite seems likely to get out of control, and crash.

6 Wear gloves in MODERATE or STRONG winds to protect your hands from line burns. This happens when the kite pulls the line through your hand so fast that the friction causes the line to heat up and burn your fingers.

Wind conditions

Try to gauge the wind speed before flying, as the most favorable winds (between 5 and 15mph) allow kites to fly most successfully. To help you gauge wind speed, use the following guide:

4-7mph
Leaves rustle, weathervanes move
LIGHT

8-12mph
Twigs and leaves in motion, flags flap
GENTLE

13-18mph
Dust swirls, small branches move
MODERATE

19-24mph
Small trees sway, waves break
FRESH

Any wind faster than 25mph makes flying difficult. On the weather forecast, a 25mph wind is termed STRONG. This wind speed will break most kites.

The most favorable wind speed for each kite is listed in the instructions.

Places to fly
Find a large, flat area away from buildings and trees. The best place is somewhere where the wind will settle down to a steady flow without any turbulence. Beaches and the windward side of smooth hills, as well as treeless areas in parks and unoccupied sports fields, are good places.

Adjustments for wind conditions
1. Launching
In the correct winds, the kites in this book should all fly straight from an outstretched arm. Lift the flying line above your head to put the kite into less turbulent air. Let the line out steadily as the kite lifts, maintaining a gentle tension. If there is not enough wind for a hand launch, a "high start" might make it possible to get the kite into fresher winds

higher up. You will need a friend to walk the kite away from you about 100 feet down wind. Let the wind fill the kite and, on your command, tell your friend to let go as you wind or pull the line in toward you. (Don't run backward, as you will not be able to see what is happening!) Keep the tension on until the kite gains some height, then quickly let out the line so that the kite floats back toward the ground. You should have more than 100 feet of line out before the kite nears the ground, when you will have to start reeling in the line again to get the kite to rise. Repeat this until the kite reaches a strong enough wind higher up. In FRESH winds the problem is to get the kite down – as you wind in the line, the kite thinks the wind speed has increased! On these occasions it helps to move toward the kite as you wind in the line.

2. Bridling
The Paper Serpent, Silver Eddy, Patchwork Three-stick Hexagonal, and Bat Box all have adjustable bridle legs. (The bridle is the line attached to the kite on

which the towing ring is secured by a lark's head hitch knot.) This allows you to vary the angle that the kite flies into the wind and thus make allowance for a variety of wind speeds. The adjustments are made in the length of the front leg between the kite and the towing ring. Adjustments should be made in small steps of ¼-½in. To help a kite fly in the stronger winds of its range, the front leg of the bridle should be shortened. In low winds, the front leg of the bridle should be lengthened.

The Frilly Delta has no bridle line but has a keel with three small holes at ½in intervals which give the adjustment. Attach the flying line to the front hole for MODERATE winds, and the back one for LIGHT winds. The central hole is for GENTLE winds.

The Stained Glass Sled does not have any adjustment forward or backward, as it alters its angle automatically to suit the wind conditions.

3. Stability

In MODERATE to FRESH winds, a kite's stability will benefit from the addition of a long tail attached to the rear of the fabric. This helps to keep the kite steady when gusts of wind come along. Experiment with streamers or chains made of paper or plastic. The rotating drag for the Silver Eddy can be used for all the kites. An increase in the bowing of the Patchwork Three-stick Hexagonal, Silver Eddy, and Bat Box will also improve the stability of these kites in gusty conditions.

Now all you have to do is attach the flying line to a swivel clip with a bowline knot, hook the clip onto the towing ring or hole of your kite and off into the sky with it. Happy flying!

A Stained Glass Sled

This is a version of a flexible kite invented in 1950 by an American, W.M. Allison. It is very simple to make and there is little to break when flying. The Stained Glass Sled will fly in LIGHT, GENTLE, and MODERATE winds, and survive in FRESH winds if you are lucky.

You will need a plastic trash can liner or garbage bag which, when cut open, gives you a sheet of plastic 2½ ft x 2¼ ft (any color will do but use a light one if you want to decorate it as shown), two ¼ in diameter ramin dowels (2¼ ft in length), sticky tape (colored or clear), 6½ ft of strong thread, felt-tip pens, a towing ring, scissors, 3 ft straight edge, a pin, and a tape measure or ruler.

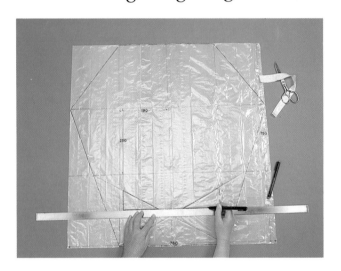

1 Cut the plastic bag to measure 2½ ft x 2¼ ft. Lay it on a flat surface and, using a felt-tip pen, mark out the shapes shown. Each rectangle should measure 7½ in x 9¾ in. The straight edge is shown positioned halfway up the bottom row of rectangles.

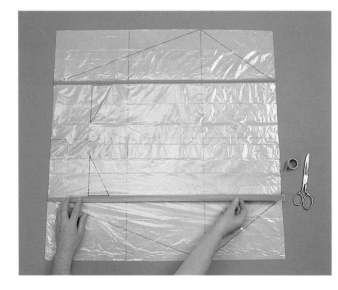

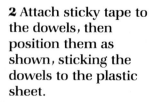

2 Attach sticky tape to the dowels, then position them as shown, sticking the dowels to the plastic sheet.

3 Using the felt-tip pens, decorate the kite surface between the dowels (except for the two triangles which will be cut out). This kite has been colored to look like a stained glass window, but you can decorate it in any way you wish.

4 Cut out the two triangles and along the outside line.

5 Reinforce the corners with two layers of tape and, using the pin, pierce a hole in each for the thread.

6 Using bowline knots, tie each end of the thread to the two reinforced holes. Hang the kite by the thread to find its center, then join it to the towing ring with a lark's head hitch knot.

7 The kite is now
ready to fly.

A Paper Serpent

The traditional covering for this ancient kite design from Thailand was paper or silk. It looks spectacular and, when flying, its paper tail makes a rustling noise. It will fly in LIGHT to MODERATE winds.

You will need ten sheets of tissue paper (five each of two colors), scraps of tissue paper for decoration, four ¼ in diameter ramin dowels (two x 2¼ ft in length, one x 2 ft, one x 1 ft), 4¾ in flexible plastic tube (¼ in internal diameter), 10 feet of strong thread, a towing ring, adhesive (UHU), spray mount, sticky tape (clear), scissors, a pin, and a tape measure.

1 Cut three pieces of plastic tube, each 1½ in in length.

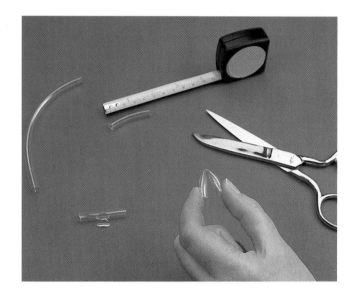

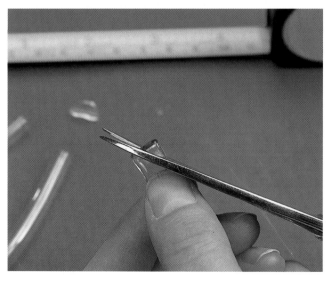

2 Cut out a section in the middle of each tube to make jointing pieces.

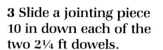

3 Slide a jointing piece 10 in down each of the two 2¼ ft dowels.

4 Join the two dowels together with the third piece of plastic tube. If any of the jointing pieces seems loose on the dowel, secure it with sticky tape.

5 Join the two dowels together by inserting the 1 ft dowel into the jointing pieces. Tie the ends of the dowels 1½ ft apart with two half hitch knots, using strong thread, looping it around one end of the 2 ft dowel exactly in the middle.

6 The other end of the 2 ft central dowel should be taped into the plastic joint at the apex of the frame.

7 Lay the dowel framework on a sheet of tissue paper and cut out the shape, leaving a ½ in border all around.

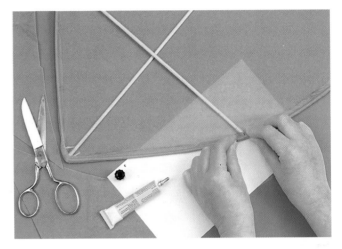

8 Glue the tissue to the dowels around the outside edges.

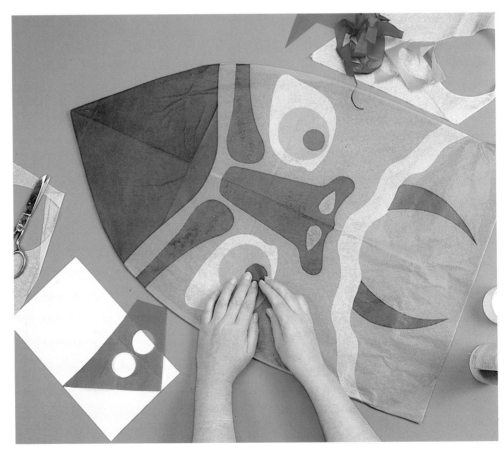

9 Create a serpent's face from the scraps of tissue paper. Glue the face on to the side of the kite without the dowels, using spray mount.

10 Ask an adult to help you with the spray mount.

11 Attach two pieces of sticky tape to the central dowel on the back of the kite, at 5¾ in and 1¾ ft from the top. Using the pin, pierce holes through both pieces of tape on either side of the central dowel.

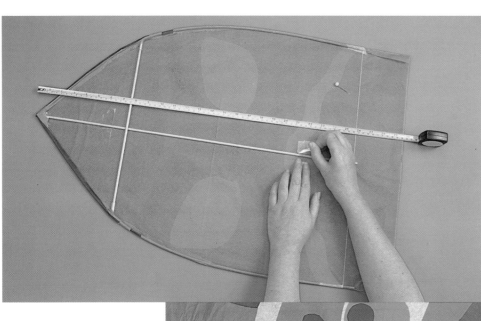

12 Take 6½ feet of the strong thread and tie each end through one set of holes. Work from the front of the kite, using a bowline knot to form the bridle. Fit the towing ring to the bridle using a lark's head hitch knot.

13 Adjust the bridle's position until the front of the kite hangs 7 in from a level surface, while the back just touches it.

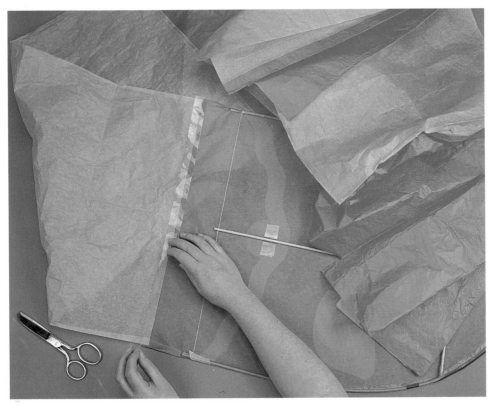

14 Glue or tape the remaining nine sheets of tissue paper to the kite, end to end, to make the tail.

15 The kite is now
ready to fly.

A Silver Eddy

William A. Eddy, an American, reinvented this stable flying kite for the western world at the beginning of this century. A similar kite has been known in Malaysia since ancient times. The Silver Eddy will fly in LIGHT to FRESH winds with or without the pinwheels and tail spinner.

You will need 1 square yard of silver plastic sheet, two ¼ in diameter ramin dowels (3 ft in length), 11½ ft of flying line, sticky tape (colored and clear), two hand-held pinwheels, a disposable plastic or paper cup, a small swivel clip, a towing ring, strong thread, a button or line tensioner, a set square (the corner of a sheet of 8½ in x 11 in paper will do), a hand drill, a 2mm drill bit, a tape measure, a pin, 3 ft straight edge, scissors, a modeling knife, and a felt-tip pen.

1 Drill one hole 1 in in from each end of one of the dowels. Ask an adult to help you with the drilling.

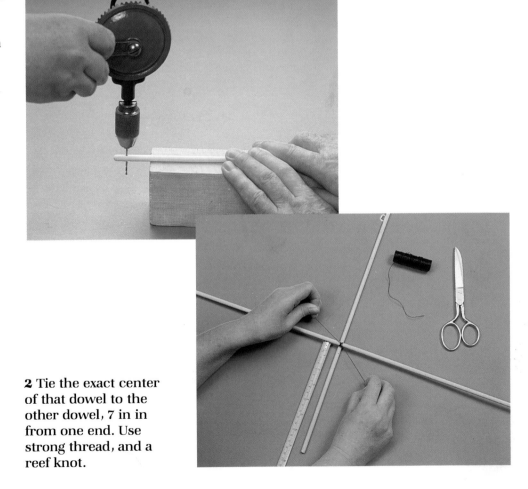

2 Tie the exact center of that dowel to the other dowel, 7 in in from one end. Use strong thread, and a reef knot.

3 Lay the plastic sheet on a flat surface. Attach clear tape to the undrilled dowel, then stick it down in a central position on the plastic sheet, with the drilled cross-spar at the top.

4 Using the set square, set the spars at right-angles to each other. Attach the drilled spar to the plastic sheet, with 10 in of tape at each end.

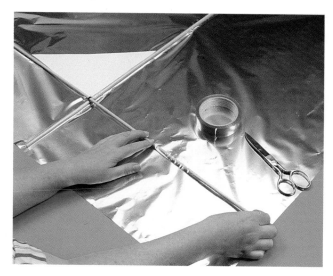

5 Measure 1 in in from the ends of the drilled dowel, as shown. Use these three points and the short end of the cross dowel to mark out the outline of the kite. Cut out the kite from the sheet.

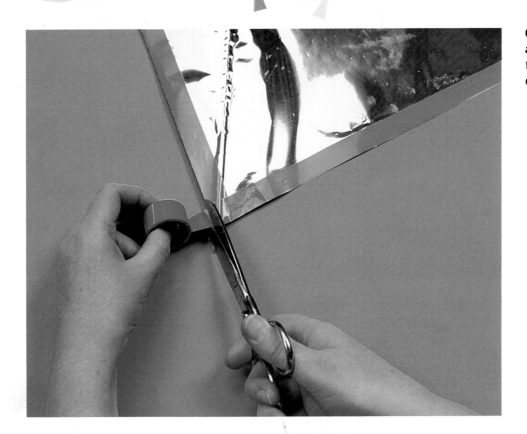

6 Turn the kite over and use colored sticky tape to reinforce the edges.

7 Using the pin, pierce a hole on either side of the central dowel in two places. The first set of holes should be where the dowels cross; the second set 1½ ft further down. To form the bridle, tie 6½ feet of flying line through the holes (and around the dowel and the crossed dowels) using bowline knots.

8 Attach the towing ring to the bridle using a lark's head hitch knot, and adjust its position so that the kite hangs with its top 1 ft from a level surface. The bottom of the kite should just touch the surface.

9 Take 5 feet of flying line and tie one end through one of the holes in the cross dowel, using a bowline knot. Thread the other end through both holes in the button or line tensioner, through the second hole in the dowel, then back to the button or line tensioner. Tie off this end with another bowline knot. Tighten the line with the tensioner to give a bow to the cross dowel. (The measurement from the line to the center of the bowed dowel should be 6 in.)

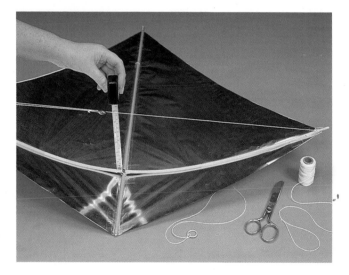

10 Cut the handles of the pinwheels to 1 in and tape them to the ends of the bowed cross dowel. Make sure they point forward at the same angle.

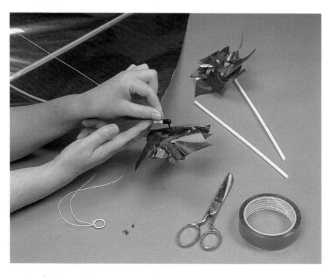

11 Cut the base from the plastic or paper cup, and mark four equidistant points around its top edge. Cut four "spinner blades", and bend them out. Decorate the cup by taping four ¼ in x 12 in strips of silver plastic, left over from the plastic sheet, to the narrow end.

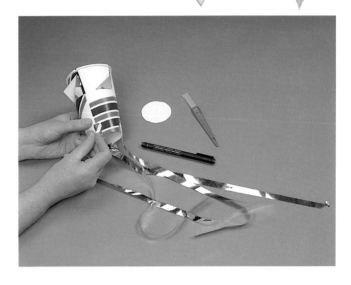

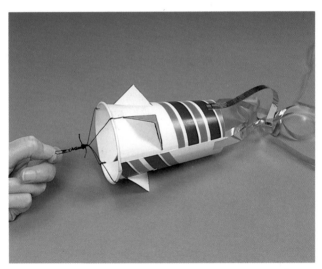

12 Take four 4 in pieces of strong thread and tie one end of each to the swivel clip using two half hitch knots. Tape the other ends equidistantly around the cup's top edge.

13 Using a bowline knot, tie a loop in a 2 ft piece of thread. Attach the other end to the kite with sticky tape wrapped around the dowel. Clip the swivel through the loop.

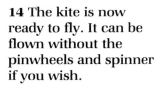

14 The kite is now ready to fly. It can be flown without the pinwheels and spinner if you wish.

A Patchwork Three-stick Hexagonal

This kite originated in China, but there are also well-known versions in Bermuda and America. It can be flown flat in LIGHT winds, or slightly bowed in MODERATE winds. It needs a long tail to stabilize its darting motion. The tail shown here is made from a bunch of paper streamers, but alternatives like paper chains, loops, and a string of bows all work well. The longer the streamers, the more stable the kite will be.

You will need one light-colored sheet of tissue paper (1½ ft x 2½ ft), two brightly colored sheets of tissue paper for the tail (1½ ft x 2½ ft), scraps of tissue paper for decoration, four ¼ in diameter ramin dowels (one x 2 ft, two x 1¾ ft, one x 2 in), sticky tape (clear), strong thread, spray mount, adhesive (UHU), a towing ring, a small swivel clip, cardboard, a small file, a tape measure, scissors, a compass, a pencil, a pin, a ruler, and a small weight (a rubber eraser will do).

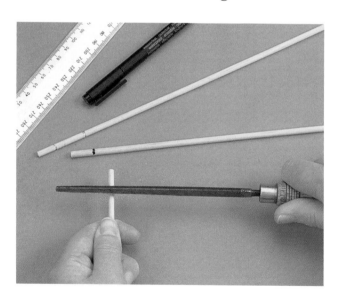

1 Measure ½ in from both ends of each of the three long dowels and file a notch. On the 2 ft dowel, you should also measure 1½ in from each end and file a second notch.

2 Tie the three sticks together at their center using strong thread and a reef knot.

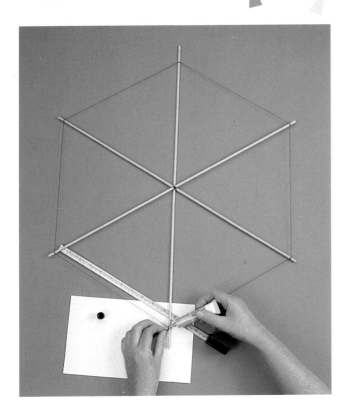

3 Using two half hitch knots, tie one end of a 6½ ft piece of strong thread to one of the inner notches on the 2 ft dowel. Using half hitch knots, tie the thread symmetrically to all the dowels at their notches so that the distance between the notches is 11 in. Glue all the knots in position once the spars are equally spaced.

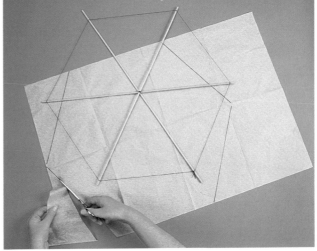

4 Place the dowels on the light-colored sheet of tissue paper and cut out the shape, leaving a ½ in border all around.

5 Glue the tissue to the thread around the outside edges.

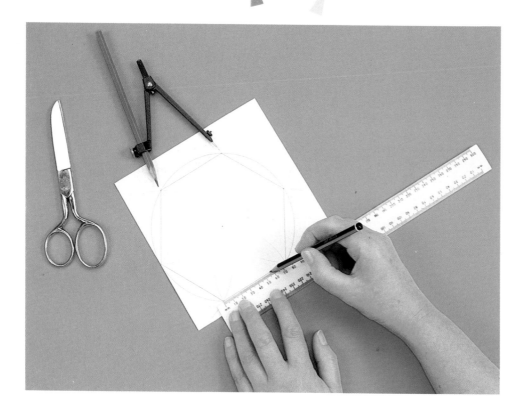

6 Draw a hexagon on the piece of cardboard, using a 3 in radius circle as its basis. Cut out the shape.

7 Using the cardboard hexagon as a template, cut out several hexagons from the tissue paper scraps. Attach them to the main hexagon with spray mount, to form a decorative pattern. (They should be positioned on the opposite side to the dowels.) The hexagons should overlap slightly in order to strengthen the surface of the kite. Ask an adult to help you with the spray mount (see photo 10 on page 17).

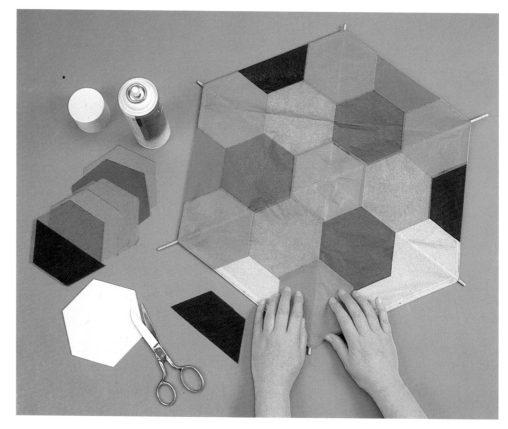

8 Using sticky tape, reinforce the corners of the tissue where the dowels stick out. You should also reinforce the tissue at the center of the kite, where the dowels cross and, with the pin, pierce a hole on either side of the longest dowel.

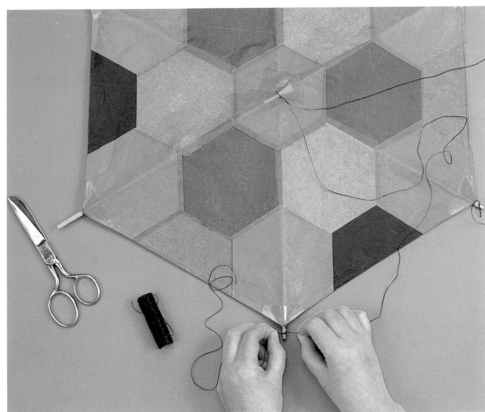

9 Thread a 6½ ft length of thread through the two holes and, using two half hitch knots, tie each end of the thread to the two dowels shown.

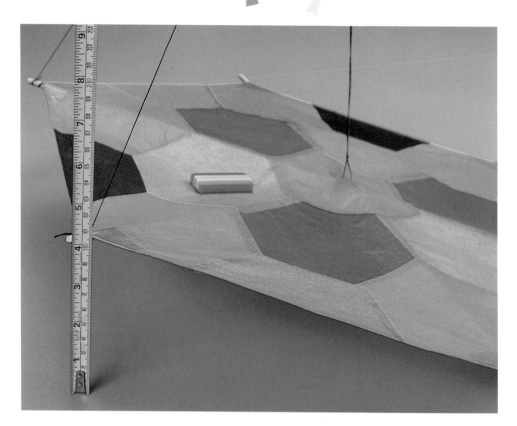

10 Loop the towing ring to this thread using a lark's head hitch knot, and adjust, until the front of the kite is 4¼ in from a flat surface, while the back just touches it. Place a small weight on the kite to keep the threads tight.

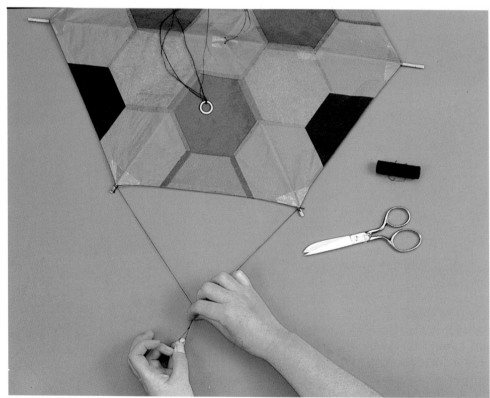

11 Tie 1½ in of thread to the ends of the opposite two dowels using two half hitch knots. Tie a half hitch in the middle of the thread to form a small loop.

12 Make the tail by cutting strips of tissue paper (1½ in wide) from the two brightly colored sheets. Glue pairs of strips end to end until you have ten strips, each 5 feet long. Gather these together, then glue them to the center of a 2¼ in length of dowel.

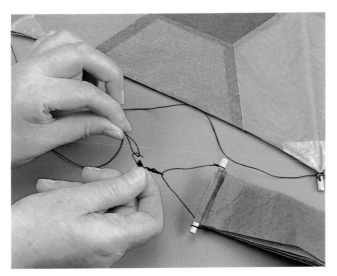

13 Take an 8 in length of thread and thread it through the swivel clip. Using two half hitch knots, tie each end to the 2¼ in length of dowel. Clip the tail to the small loop.

14 To bow the kite for extra stability in moderate winds, take a length of strong thread and tie a loop with a bowline knot at each end so that the loops are 2 ft apart. You might need to try this a few times before you get the measurement right. The thread can then be hooked onto the two outside notches on the longest dowel to give the required bow to the kite.

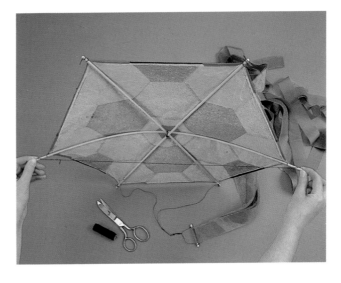

15 The kite is now
ready to fly.

This is a fine, soaring, flexible kite that was invented by Francis M. Rogallo in the United States. It will fly in LIGHT, GENTLE, and MODERATE winds, and if cut down to the basic Delta (that is, without the frills shown here), it will float gently down when the wind drops to nothing and may still be flying when the next breeze arrives to make it rise again.

You will need two plastic trash can liners (each one a different color), four ¼ in diameter ramin dowels (two x 2¾ ft in length, one x 2½ ft, one x 2 ft), masking tape or sticky tape (colored), sticky tape (clear), three eyelets, 3 in flexible plastic tubing (6mm internal diameter), a piece of cardboard 2¼ ft x 4 in, scissors, 3 ft straight edge, a tape measure or ruler, a hole punch, a modeling knife, a cutting board, a small hacksaw, and a felt-tip pen.

1 Cut off the bottom of one of the colored trash can liners. Cut down one side, too, to give you a flat sheet. Fold this sheet back and forth to make eight layers of plastic on which the cardboard can be laid.

Using the modeling knife and cutting board, cut around the cardboard to give you eight equal strips of plastic sheet. Do the same with the other colored trash can liner.

2 Tape alternate colors of the strips together with the colored sticky tape or masking tape. Allow a 4 in "step" between each strip. Build up seven strips with the steps going down to the left, and seven strips with the steps going down to the right.

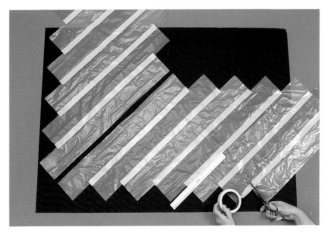

3 You should have two strips of plastic left. Cut a square (4 in x 4 in) from one strip and, using clear tape, join it to the other.

4 Using the long strip (which should now measure 2½ ft x 4 in) as the center piece, join the two sets of strips together – one set on either side.

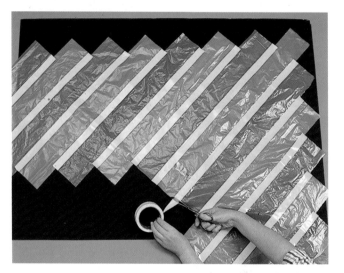

5 Trim off the triangle shapes at the edges, as shown. Make two 1½ in jointing pieces from the plastic tubing by bending them and cutting out a section from the middle (see photos 1 and 2 on page 14).

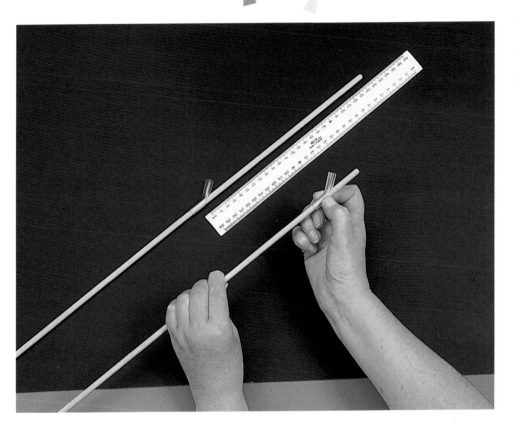

6 Take the two 2¾ ft dowels and slide a plastic jointing piece onto each, 9½ in down from one end.

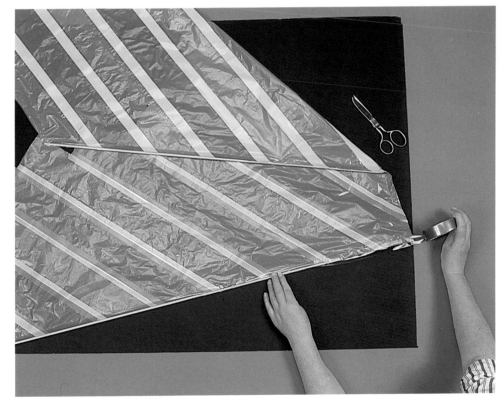

7 Turn the kite over and, using clear tape, attach the dowels to the plastic sheet in the positions shown. The plastic jointing pieces should point toward the center of the kite. Use sticky tape to reinforce the edge of the unsupported plastic sheet from the dowels to the point of the kite.

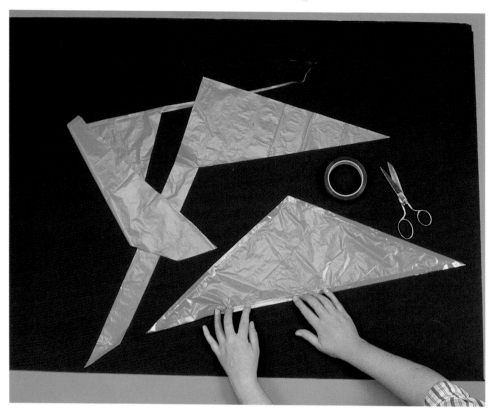

8 Make a keel from two sheets of plastic taped together. The keel should measure 2½ ft x 1½ ft x 1¼ ft.

9 Reinforce the obtuse angle of the keel with extra tape on both sides, and position the three holes ¼ in apart.

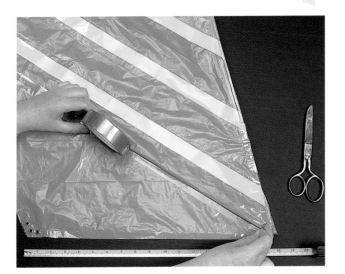

10 Fold the kite in half, with the colored tape outside. Attach the keel to the center of the kite along the 2½ ft side. Attach it on both sides so that the 1½ ft side is nearest to the point of the kite.

11 Tape the 2½ ft dowel to the center of the kite, on the opposite side to the keel.

12 Carefully try to insert the 2 ft dowel into the plastic jointing pieces. It should be too long. Shorten it until it is possible to assemble it without straining the plastic sheeting. When attached, the sheeting should be loose.

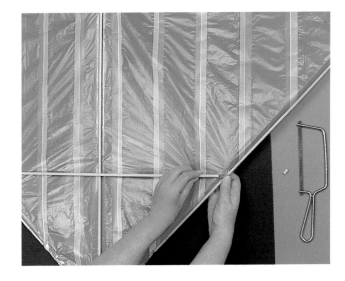

13 The kite is now ready to fly.

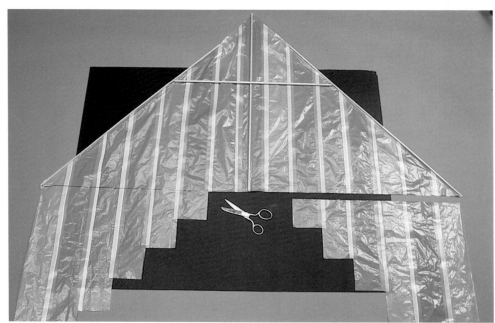

14 To fly the kite without the frills, simply cut them off along the black line as shown.

A Bat Box

This is a kite developed from the French Military Box, which was invented before World War I. It was used for flying a rescue line ashore from a boat that had been blown onto rocks by a storm. This kite will, therefore, fly in STRONG winds. GENTLE, MODERATE, and FRESH winds will suit it best, but some excitement can be had in winds above 25mph as it is the most stable of the six kites in the book.

You will need a black trash can liner, colored scraps of plastic sheet (shopping bags will do), five ¼ in diameter ramin dowels (three x 3 ft in length, one x 2 ft, one x 1¾ ft), sticky tape (clear and colored), 10 feet of flying line, a towing ring, a line tensioner, strong thread, a sheet of cardboard (1¾ ft x 1½ ft), scissors, a tape measure or ruler, a modeling knife, a cutting board, a pin, a hand drill, a 2mm drill bit, and a felt-tip pen.

1 Cut off the bottom of the trash can liner. Cut down one side, too, to give you a flat sheet. Cut out a piece 3 ft x 2¾ ft and lay it on a flat surface. Take two of the 3 ft ramin dowels and tape them centrally to the plastic sheet, 8 in apart. Drill a hole 2mm in diameter, ½ in in from each end of the remaining 3 ft dowel. Ask an adult to help you with the drilling (see photo 1 on page 20).

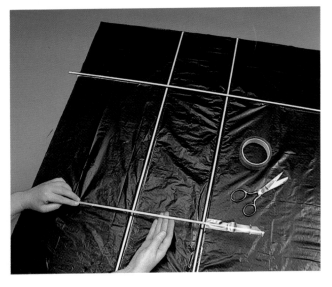

2 Using the felt-tip pen, make a mark on the two 3 ft dowels 9¾ in in from each end. Tape the drilled dowel to the plastic over one pair of marks on the parallel dowels. Use 8 in of sticky tape at each end of the drilled dowel. (Make allowance for the dowel's 1¼ in overlap of the plastic at each end.) Tape the 1¾ ft dowel centrally over the other two marks with 4 in of tape at each end.

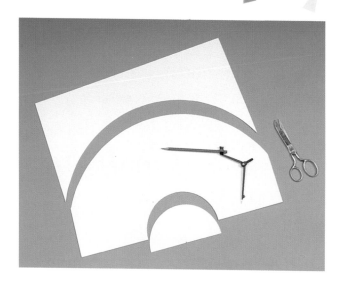

3 Cut two pieces of cardboard that have radii of 11¾ in and 3¾ in respectively. These will be used as guides.

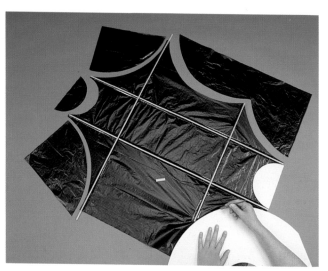

4 Place the plastic sheet on the cutting board. Using the modeling knife and the guides, cut out the shape shown.

5 Using the pin, pierce a hole through the plastic on either side of the dowels where they cross. Tie each set of crossed dowels together using reef knots and strong thread.

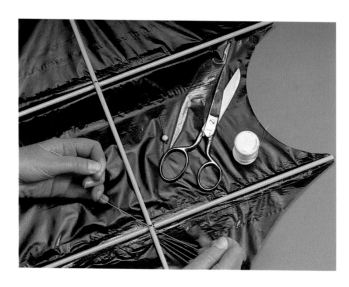

6 Take two pieces of plastic sheet measuring 8 in x 1¼ ft and tape them to the 2 ft dowel centrally, as shown, to make the half box.

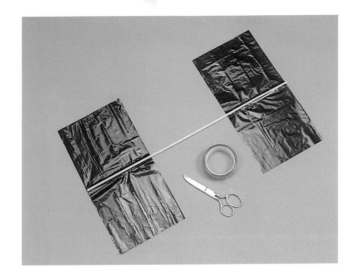

7 Turn the kite over so that the dowels are underneath. Measure 6 in down from the top of the parallel dowels (the drilled dowel should be uppermost) and tape the ends of the 8 in x 1¼ ft sheets over the dowels (inside *and* out) to attach the half box. You will need help to position the last two pieces of tape, as the 2 ft dowel will have to be lifted while the tapes are put in place.

8 Cut out a panel 7 in x 9¾ in between the parallel dowels and where the half box is attached, as shown.

9 Using sticky tape, reinforce the plastic sheet around the 2 ft dowel of the half box 2 in down from the top, and 5¾ in up from the bottom. Pierce a hole on either side of the dowel, through the reinforcing.

10 Thread 5 feet of flying line through one pair of holes and tie a bowline knot. Thread the other end through the remaining holes and tie off as before. To make the bridle, attach the towing ring to the bridle using a lark's head hitch.

11 Using colored tape or pieces of plastic sheet, decorate the kite with some spooky features. Hang the kite from the towing ring above a level surface and adjust its position until the front of the kite is 9 in above the surface, while the back just touches it (see photo 13 on page 18).

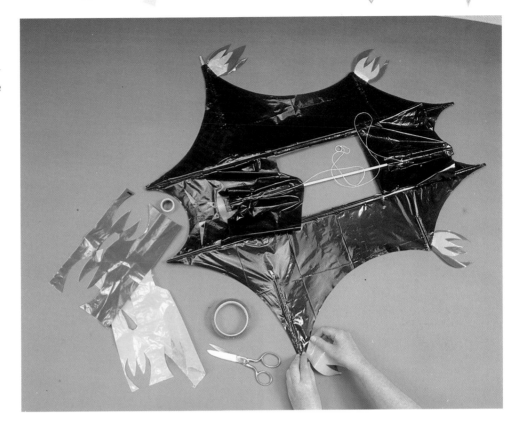

12 Take 5 ft of line and attach it to the drilled dowel and line tensioner. See photo 9 on page 23. Adjust the tensioner to bow the dowel until the line is 6 in from the dowel at the center.

13 The kite is now
ready to fly, but do
add two long tails to
the parallel dowels if
you try to fly the kite
in strong winds!

Stationery, office supply and crafts stores carry most of the items listed in this book such as tissue paper, felt-tip pens, hole punches, adhesives, and sticky tape. Plastic garbage bags can be found at supermarkets, and more colorful plastic bags from retailers. Hand-held pinwheels are found at toy stores. Thread, buttons, and eyelets at the notions counter of fabric stores. Artists' supply stores carry silver mylar sheets and spray mount. Many hardware stores carry wood dowel rods and flexible plastic tubing. (If your hardware store doesn't have tubing, the aquarium store will.)

More specialized items, such as flying line, handles, reels, etc., are found in shops specializing in materials for kites. If you have a hobby shop nearby, check with them first. They may stock everything you need. The following merchants specialize in selling kites and kite building materials by mail:

Into the Wind
1408-D Pearl Street
Boulder, CO 80302
(303) 449-5356

High Fly Kite Co.
30 West End Ave.
Haddonfield, NJ 08033
(609) 429-6260

Magazines

American Kite
Quarterly – $10.00 per year
480 Clementina St.
San Francisco, CA 94103

KiteLines
Quarterly – $12.00 per year
P.O. Box 466
Randallstown, MD 21133

Kiting – Journal of the American Kitefliers Association
Bi-monthly – free with membership
1559 Rockville Pike
Rockville, MD 20852

Clubs

American Kitefliers Association
1559 Rockville Pike
Rockville, MD 20852
$15.00 per year dues

The first kites were invented approximately 2,000 years ago in China, but it is difficult to be absolutely sure of the date. It would be nice to think that a child built the first kite after nearly being blown into the sky holding on to the clothing which he or she had been attempting to hang on the washing line! It is more likely that kites evolved from the large marching banners and windsocks used by armies to advertise their presence and to impress the enemy. Kites were able to fly higher and thus be more impressive. They could fly at night over an enemy encampment scaring the soldiers with the wails and moans of their hummers. (Hummers were made with a piece of stiff paper attached to a tight string strung across the spars).

The long history of kite flying can be divided into three main periods, each corresponding to changes which occurred in the kites' structure and materials. First, there were the flat, inelastic, sometimes bowed, structures which were developed in Asia. They were made of silk, paper, and bamboo. Second, in the nineteenth century, three dimensional, cloth-covered, box-like forms became dominant, and the use of bowed or dihedral spars was commonplace. Last, since World War II, designers have used new plastic materials to create flexible structures and flying surfaces.

Early kites required expensive silk coverings over bamboo spars, and so were not generally available to everybody. When paper could be produced cheaply and religious groups began to make use of kites for their festivals, many more people could build kites and fly their own offerings to their gods. One example of this is the Chinese fertility, or rice, kite made in the shape of three grains of rice. It is flown over paddy fields with rice stalks attached to its wing tips and tail. The wind shaking the rice grains from the kite and onto the ground below symbolizes fertility and an abundant harvest. Koreans also have a traditional use for kites. At the start of each new year, the name and date of birth of each male child are written on a paper kite that is flown in the sky. At its highest, it is let go, taking away the evil spirits that might have influenced the child's future.

Kite making and ancient kite festivals are known in all the countries surrounding China, in Japan, Indonesia, Malaysia, Korea, and India, but kite flying was not introduced to Europe until the fifteenth century. It was probably brought to Europe by Dutch traders.

For a long time, it was thought of only as a child's toy. It was not until 1752 that the first of many scientific kite experiments was made. Benjamin Franklin made a kite out of a large silk handkerchief, and flew it during a thunderstorm and proved that the discharge of electricity from lightning was the same as that generated by a machine in a laboratory. Many more experiments followed and with the development of man-lifting kites, their military use was rediscovered. Kites at this time were covered with linen or cotton fabric.

During World War I, the American, Samuel Franklin Cody, one of the foremost designers of that period, was made Chief Kite Instructor to the British War Office. Huge Cody kites were used to lift a man from a warship or submarine to spot enemy ships over the horizon. These were soon replaced by balloons and airplanes. Incidentally, Cody was also the first man in Britain to build and fly an airplane. The term "kite" used for an airplane probably derives from this time when a plane was really only a kite with an engine.

The most significant of recent developments in kite design is the flexible kite, invented and patented in 1948 by Francis Rogallo. It has proved to be very useful in the American space program, for bringing capsules back to earth. It is also the basis for most of the early hanggliders of today (being derivatives of the Delta kite).

With the invention of modern, strong, lightweight, and colorful materials, there has been a huge revival of interest in kite flying, and a wide variety of new designs for the individual to fly.

PRINTED IN BELGIUM BY

INTERNATIONAL BOOK PRODUCTION

DATE DUE

DEC 4 1996		
FEB 13 1997		
FEB 13 1997		
FEB 13 1997		
FEB 13 1997		
MAR 13 1998		
OCT 20 2000 DEC 14 2000		
NOV 14 2001		

HIGHSMITH #45231